Studying Vocabulary

1

PRESTWICK
H O U S E
INCORPORATED

P.O. Box 246 • Cheswold, DE 19936
Tel: 1.800.932.4593
Web site: www.prestwickhouse.com

ISBN: 1-58049-250-9

TABLE OF CONTENTS

Lesson One 4

Lesson Two 6

Lesson Three 8

Lesson Four 10

Lesson Five...12

Lesson Six...14

Lesson Seven 16

Lesson Eight 18

Lesson Nine2...0

Lesson Ten 22

Lesson Eleven 24

Lesson Twelve 26

Lesson Thirteen..28

Lesson Fourteen 30

Lesson Fifteen 3..2

Lesson Sixteen 34

Lesson Seventeen 36

Lesson Eighteen..38

Lesson Nineteen 40

Lesson Twenty 42

Lesson Twenty-One 44

Lesson Twenty-Two 46

Lesson Twenty-Three 48

Lesson Twenty-Four 50

Lesson Twenty-Five 52

Lesson Twenty-Six 54

Lesson Twenty-Seven 56

Lesson Twenty-Eight 58

Mini-dictionary 60

To The Student

We have entitled our book STUDYING VOCABULARY because we believe at some point in his or her school career, each student must sit down and work at committing selected words and their definitions to memory. One of the purposes of this book and the available testing program is to encourage you to learn to do so.

Of course, anyone could memorize any word and its definition for the short term, but we want these words to stay with you for the rest of your life, so we have done the following:

- We have chosen high-frequency words that are generally found in everyday reading material and in the speech of the average person. In this way, your learning of these words and definitions should be reinforced and made easier.
- In the event that you do not read very much, however, we have taken a second step. All of the quizzes in the testing program are cumulative. Each week you will be asked to identify the definition of the new words *plus* various review words, because they will be included in the following lessons.

LESSON ONE

Exercise I

In your own words, write a brief definition for as many words on the list as you can. Then correct and/or complete the lesson by using the mini-dictionary in the back of this book.

1. armored
2. consult
3. deterioration
4. eavesdropping
5. embarrassment
6. evacuate
7. extensive
8. inexpensive
9. interception
10. mutual
11. predictions
12. ransom
13. residents
14. sightings
15. welcome

Exercise II

From the list of words, fill in the blanks to make complete sentences.

1. Richard Nixon was one of many _____ to live in the White House.

2. I was filled with _____ when I tripped and fell.

3. The kidnappers sent a _____ note.

4. Mother wanted to buy a car that was _____ , but Dad's heart was set on a Cadillac.

5. The fortune-teller made many _____ about our future.

6. Because of the flood, we had to _____ our home.

7. You should _____ an attorney before starting a lawsuit.

8. There was no one at home to _____ us.

9. The divorce was obtained by _____ consent.

10. Termites, weather, and neglect had caused much _____ to the old mansion.

11. The tall football player made a terrific _____ and carried the ball seventy yards for a touchdown.

12. After very _____ testing, the scientist perfected the new drug.

13. Banks have always used _____ cars to transfer money to other institutions.

14. _____ is not always the best means of gaining information.

15. There have not been as many _____ of UFOs reported in the news lately.

Exercise III

Study the following roots, prefixes, and suffixes and then answer the questions. Consider the literal meaning of each word.

in –	A prefix meaning:	*not*
dict –	A root meaning:	*to speak, to tell*
pre –	A prefix meaning:	*before*
tion –	A suffix meaning:	*the act of*

1. The literal meaning of the word "prediction" is _____.

2. One word meaning not correct is _____.

3. A dictator is one who _____.

4. One word meaning "not active" is _____.

5. One word meaning "not audible" is _____.

6. A dictaphone is a machine you _____.

7. The word "diction" has to do with a _____.

8. If you predate a check, you are writing a _____.

9. A prefix comes _____.

10. A prehistoric animal is one that lived _____.

LESSON TWO

Exercise I

In your own words, write a brief definition for as many words on the list as you can. Then correct and/or complete the lesson by using the mini-dictionary in the back of this book.

1. accident

2. critical

3. curator

4. defective

5. discussion

6. disgusting

7. hamper

8. identical

9. international

10. irrigation

11. legitimate

12. materialize

13. opponent

14. possibility

15. produce (noun)

Exercise II

From the list of words, fill in the blanks to make complete sentences.

1. His _____ in his last fight knocked him out of the ring.

2. We made a _____ offer for the property, but the real estate salesman laughed.

3. An underground _____ system kept the garden properly watered.

4. After a lengthy _____, the attorneys decided to settle out of court.

5. We bought some _____ , which included spinach, carrots, and onions.

6. Quite by _____, we discovered the secret path leading to the cabin.

7.   According to the inspector, the fire was due to _____ wiring.

8.   Some scenes in the movie were so _____ that many people left early.

9.   There is a good _____ that several inches of snow will fall tonight.

10. Parents are often _____ of their children's behavior.

11. _____ reports were given by several witnesses.

12. For _____ travel, you need a passport.

13. Insufficient rest can _____ one's ability to learn.

14. The _____ of the museum discovered that the painting was fake.

15. It's easy for a good magician to make coins _____ out of thin air.

Exercise III

Study the following roots, prefixes, and suffixes and then answer the questions. Consider the literal meaning of each word.

inter –	A prefix meaning:	1. *between; among*
		2. *mutually; together*
ject –	A root meaning:	*to throw*

1.   If you inject a poison, you are _____.

2.   If you interject a comment, you are _____.

3.   If you reject a suggestion, you are _____.

4.   If you project your voice, you are _____.

5.   If you are feeling dejected, you are _____.

6.   If you have feelings of rejection, you are _____.

7.   An international treaty is a _____.

8.   An intercontinental plane flight is a _____.

9.   If you intercede in an argument between your father and brother, you are _____ _____.

10. If there is a good deal of interaction in the classroom, it means that _____ _____.

LESSON THREE

Exercise I

In your own words, write a brief definition for as many words on the list as you can. Then correct and/or complete the lesson by using the mini-dictionary in the back of this book.

1. accurate

2. coroner

3. entry

4. extreme

5. feverish

6. hideous

7. magnificent

8. menacing

9. mysterious

10. panic

11. plantation

12. plunge

13. serious

14. shrill

15. thorough

Exercise II

From the list of words, fill in the blanks to make complete sentences.

1. The _____ stranger disappeared into the crowd.

2. Because John was not very _____ when he cleaned, he was fired.

3. Cotton and tobacco were the main crops grown on a Southern _____.

4. In a _____ attempt to escape, the wild horse stepped on my foot.

5. The old man's _____ voice broke the silence.

6. The _____ pronounced the accident victim dead on arrival.

7.   A sudden power failure caused _____ in the crowded theater.

8.   After a quick _____ in the icy stream, the overheated campers felt refreshed.

9.   A _____ scream echoed through the halls.

10. Grand larceny is a _____ offense.

11. The dog growled in a _____ manner.

12. The temperature goes from one _____ to the other.

13. To gain _____ onto the estate, we had to show our engraved invitations.

14. The tourists viewed a _____ sunset across the canyon.

15. The witness's description was not very _____.

Exercise III

Study the following roots, prefixes, and suffixes and then answer the questions. Consider the literal meaning of each word.

mono –	A prefix meaning:	*one*
bi –	A prefix meaning:	*two or twice (bimonthly means either every two months or twice a month.)*
tri –	A prefix meaning:	*three*

1.   A bicycle is a cycle with _____ wheels.

2.   A tricycle is a cycle with _____ wheels.

3.   A train that runs on one rail is called a _____.

4.   A figure with three angles is called a _____.

5.   Someone who speaks only in one tone is said to speak in a _____.

6.   A magazine that comes biweekly comes _____.

7.   "Lingual" means language, so someone who is bilingual can _____.

8.   Monogamy is the custom of being married to only one person at a time. Someone who is guilty of bigamy is _____ .

LESSON FOUR

Exercise I

In your own words, write a brief definition for as many words on the list as you can. Then correct and/or complete the lesson by using the mini-dictionary in the back of this book.

1. ancient

2. cautiously

3. confirm

4. denied

5. domesticated

6. edible

7. emerge

8. extinct

9. fate

10. incredible

11. item

12. relief

13. soar

14. tedious

15. warrant

Exercise II

From the list of words, fill in the blanks to make complete sentences.

1. _____ animals make the best pets.

2. The bald eagle was in danger of becoming _____.

3. The police department issued a_____ for his arrest.

4. The look of _____ on her face told us how worried she had been.

5. Who will _____ as the victor in this contest?

6. The _____ ruins of the Acropolis are constantly being repaired.

7. The food was barely _____, but we managed to down a few bites.

8. No man knows what his or her _____ is going to be.

9. The car _____ edged into the crowded intersection.

10. It is better to _____ like an eagle than crawl like a snake.

11. The accused man _____ all charges brought against him.

12. The passenger had to _____ his airline reservation.

13. It was against _____ odds that we finally won the race.

14. Because his class was so _____, the boy fell asleep.

15. The _____ he stole was worth two dollars.

Exercise III

Study the following roots, prefixes, and suffixes and then answer the questions. Consider the literal meaning of each word.

fact –	A root meaning:	*to make*
mal –	A prefix meaning:	*bad, badly*
bene –	A prefix meaning:	*good, well*
mis –	A prefix meaning:	*wrong, incorrectly*

1. To spell a word incorrectly is to _____ the word.

2. Someone who does not fit in is said to be a _____.

3. Someone who makes good things happen for you is a _____.

4. A company that manufactures products is one that _____.

5. A factory is a place where products are _____.

6. A malignant tumor is one which is _____, but a benign tumor is _____.

7. If you are in bed suffering with a malady, you probably are _____.

8. If a doctor is sued for malpractice, he or she is accused of _____.

LESSON FIVE

Exercise I

In your own words, write a brief definition for as many words on the list as you can. Then correct and/or complete the lesson by using the mini-dictionary in the back of this book.

1. caution

2. fasten

3. formidable

4. harness

5. hasten

6. irritable

7. miserable

8. occupy

9. pursuit

10. sapped

11. senseless

12. snug

13. task

14. torrential

15. unruly

Exercise II

From the list of words, fill in the blanks to make complete sentences.

1   The new solar homes _____ the sun's energy for heat.

2. In the Bible, Samson's strength was _____ after his haircut.

3. A stunning blow to the head left the boxer _____.

4. After arguing bitterly, both girls felt _____.

5. Before the car is started, peopple should _____ their safety belt.

6. _____ rains finally put out the forest fire.

7. The sheriff was in hot _____ of the stolen car.

8. We were told that we could not _____ the apartment until we paid the first and last month's rent.

9. Motorists should drive with utmost _____ when the roads are icy.

10. The child was _____ after his visit with the doctor.

11. It was a difficult _____ to accomplish.

12. Goliath was a _____ opponent for little David.

13. Wild and _____ behavior will not be tolerated.

14. "The children were nestled all _____ in their beds."

15. We must _____ to the supermarket before it closes.

Exercise III

Review of Roots, Prefixes, and Suffixes.

1. Something that is inedible is _____.

2. A precaution is _____.

3. If you give your secretary dictation, you are _____.

4. If you misspeak, you have _____.

5. An intergalactic spaceship travels _____.

6. The prefix *ject* means _____.

7. The prefix *bi* means _____.

8. The prefix *mono* means _____.

9. The prefix *tri* means _____.

10. The root *fact* means _____.

11. The prefix *mal* means _____.

12. The prefix *bene* means _____.

LESSON SIX

Exercise I

In your own words, write a brief definition for as many words on the list as you can. Then correct and/or complete the lesson by using the mini-dictionary in the back of this book.

1. adoration

2. bared

3. blundered

4. clutched

5. crazed

6. discarded

7. dismal

8. glitter

9. harsh

10. injurious

11. persistent

12. savage

13. tolerant

14. wearily

15. yearning

Exercise II

From the list of words, fill in the blanks to make complete sentences.

1. After we _____ through the forest for hours, we finally came to a highway.

2. John's mother said he was _____, but other people said he was stubborn.

3. The new owner of the restaurant was not very _____ of the sloppy waitress.

4. The first-time marathon runners _____ walked the last few miles of the race.

5. Tobacco and alcohol may be _____ to your health.

6. Grandmother's eyes were full of _____ as the baby crawled towards her.

14

7. For a long time, I've had a _____ to return to my native land.

8. The law says that punishment may not be _____ or cruel.

9. Sometimes the stars _____ like diamonds.

10. The snarling beast had a _____ look about him that made us back away.

11. With the heavy coat _____ firmly around her, the girl struggled through the torrential rains.

12. Our guard dog _____ his teeth and lunged toward the intruder.

13. Many _____ items of clothing were in disorderly piles on the floor.

14. Not accustomed to being caged, the gorilla became almost _____ in his efforts to escape.

15. The _____ weather did little to cheer us.

Exercise III

(Review – Lessons 1 - 6.)
Match each word on the left to its correct definition on the right.

_____	1.	defective	A.	tiresome, boring
_____	2.	interception	B.	faulty
_____	3.	tedious	C.	untouched by civilization; wild
_____	4.	ransom	D.	the stopping or interruption of the course or progress of something
_____	5.	incredible	E.	unbelievable
_____	6.	savage	F.	a person who opposes another
_____	7.	hideous	G.	the price or payment to obtain a release
_____	8.	opponent	H.	ugly
_____	9.	formidable	I.	depleted or weakened gradually
_____	10.	yearning	J.	inspiring fear, dread, or alarm
_____	11.	sapped	K.	splendid in appearance
_____	12.	magnificent	L.	a deep longing; a desire

LESSON SEVEN

Exercise I

In your own words, write a brief definition for as many words on the list as you can. Then correct and/or complete the lesson by using the mini-dictionary in the back of this book.

1. admiration

2. annual

3. bruise

4. depart

5. disaster

6. exact

7. excess

8. illustrate

9. immobilize

10. late

11. revenge

12. reluctantly

13. soothing

14. unintentional

15. vicinity

Exercise II

From the list of words, fill in the blanks to make complete sentences.

1. If a broken leg is suspected, an effort should be made to _____ the limb.

2. An ugly, black _____ on the man's shoulder indicated he had been hit by a heavy object.

3. The attorney read the Last Will and Testament of our _____ Uncle George.

4. Drinking or eating to _____ is not healthy for anyone.

5. To _____ her point, the professor drew a diagram on the board.

6. We were in the general _____ when the alarm sounded.

7. All of the passengers were ready to _____ for their African safari.

8. It is time for my _____ dental checkup.

9. The tired soldiers _____ picked up their heavy gear and began to climb slowly into the truck.

10. The doctor's _____ words comforted the nervous patient.

11. The President declared the flooded community to be a _____ area.

12. Although it was _____, he did hit John in the nose when he went for the ball.

13. Shaking his fist in the air, the poor farmer swore to get _____ on the man who stole the prized pig.

14. As the actor took another curtain call, he was proud to see the _____ on the faces of his fans.

15. The bus driver requires that the passengers have the _____ change.

Exercise III

Analogies can take a variety of forms, but the two most common kind involve either words that mean the same or words that mean the opposite.

For example
big : large :: quick : _____
Big means the same as large, so we are looking for a word that means the same as quick.

big : small :: warm : _____
In this one, big means the opposite of small, so we are looking for a word that means the opposite of warm.

Using words from Lesson Seven, complete the following analogies.

1. wide : broad :: leave : _____

2. fat : thin :: upsetting : _____

3. street : road :: precise : _____

4. cold : warm :: eagerly : _____

5. friendly : hostile :: forgiveness: _____

Using words from earlier leassons, complete the following analogies.

6. plain : fancy :: pretty :_____

7. frequently : often :: similar : _____

8. long : short :: interesting : _____

LESSON EIGHT

Exercise I

In your own words, write a brief definition for as many words on the list as you can. Then correct and/or complete the lesson by using the mini-dictionary in the back of this book.

1. accomplishment
2. cliff
3. corpse
4. crate
5. dependable
6. grief
7. initial
8. narrate
9. neglected
10. nuisance
11. odor
12. picturesque
13. refreshing
14. simulate
15. stricken

Exercise II

From the list of words, fill in the blanks to make complete sentences.

1. Because he was not _____, the boss fired John.

2. Oranges are generally packed in a _____ for shipping.

3. It was a(n) _____ change to be out of school on a Wednesday.

4. The mountain climbers stopped on a steep _____ to check their gear.

5. Pictures and scale models of the shuttle are often used to _____ space travel.

6. Graduation from high school is a major _____ for teenagers.

18

7. Insects can be quite a(n) _____ in the summertime.

8. The policeman asked him to _____ the events leading up to the murder.

9. The explorer was _____ with disease and quickly died.

10. Palm trees, white sand, and gentle waves made a _____ setting for our picnic.

11. His _____ reaction was to fight, but his friend cooled him down.

12. A strange _____ filled the room.

13. The boy was filled with _____ when he heard that his dog had been killed.

14. The sickly baby, wrapped in rags, had been _____ by his mother.

15. An unidentified _____ was put into cold storage at the morgue.

Exercise III

Study the following roots, prefixes, and suffixes and then answer the questions. Consider the literal meaning of each word.

re –	A prefix meaning:	*again, back*
auto –	A root meaning:	*self*
ent, er, ant, ar, or –	Suffixes meaning:	*one who*
ess –	Suffix meaning:	*one who (feminine)*

1. A director is _____.

2. A hostess is _____.

3. A beggar is _____.

4. An instructor is _____.

5. A poetess is _____.

6. A conductor is _____.

7. If you call something back, you have _____ it.

8. A self-moving vehicle is _____.

9. If you design something once, then go back and design it again, you have _____ it.

LESSON NINE

Exercise I

In your own words, write a brief definition for as many words on the list as you can. Then correct and/or complete the lesson by using the mini-dictionary in the back of this book.

1. astonishing
2. flushed
3. frugally
4. glowed
5. imagination
6. inhabit
7. numbing
8. occupants
9. partially
10. personnel
11. pessimistic
12. raging
13. resemble
14. standard
15. tolerate

Exercise II

From the list of words, fill in the blanks to make complete sentences.

1. Our parents and teachers will not _____ rudeness.

2. Having been forced to retire, the old foreman was _____ about his future.

3. A novelist needs a vivid _____ to be able to write a best-selling book.

4. Although they were twins, they did not _____ each other.

5. Job applications are normally sent to the _____ office.

6. Spiders and mice were the only _____ of the cave.

7. The old miser _____ counted out a few coins and gave them to the boy.

8. Candles _____ softly in the windows as a welcome to visitors.

9. The runner's face was _____ from all the exercise.

10. A dose of castor oil used to be the _____ cure for many ailments.

11. It was _____ for such a small child to be that intelligent.

12. The shot the dentist injected had a _____ effect on Stacy's jaw.

13. A _____ eaten sandwich lay on the counter.

14. Thoughts raced through my mind, much like the _____ storm outside.

15. Some birds will _____ a deserted nest.

Exercise III

Study the following roots, prefixes, and suffixes and then answer the questions. Consider the literal meaning of each word.

ee –	A suffix meaning:	*one who is*
gram, graph –	A root meaning:	*to write*
tele –	A prefix meaning:	*over a distance*

1. If you send a written message over a distance, you have sent a _____.

2. Pirates could see over a distance by using a _____.

3. A counselor counsels a _____.

4. An employer employs an _____.

5. If you pay someone, he or she is the _____.

6. A court stenographer _____.

LESSON TEN

Exercise I

In your own words, write a brief definition for as many words on the list as you can. Then correct and/or complete the lesson by using the mini-dictionary in the back of this book.

1. acquaintances

2. brilliantly

3. contented

4. disguise

5. efficient

6. entries

7. frail

8. imitation

9. intent

10. leisurely

11. navigate

12. retreat

13. tattered

14. unbearably

15. urging

Exercise II

From the list of words, fill in the blanks to make complete sentences.

1. You will be more _____ if you first plan your work.

2. Sugar helped to _____ the bitter taste of the coffee.

3. The moon and stars shone _____ to light our path toward home.

4. He was so _____ in his reading, that he did not notice that the bus left without him.

5. The necklace was a cheap _____ of the priceless original.

6. I have many _____, but only a few good friends.

7. The ship's captain made many _____ in his logbook.

8. It took a lot of _____ to persuade the youngster to climb onto the horse's back.

9. An old, _____ sweater was wrapped around his _____ shoulders.

10. With a _____ purr, the cat stretched lazily on the sofa.

11. It was _____ hot in the steaming jungle.

12. After a _____ stroll around the park, we returned home.

13. The disorganized gang beat a hasty _____ into the hills.

14. After a long night of avoiding coral reefs and high winds, the captain told the young sailor to _____ the ship along the coast.

Exercise III

Study the following roots, prefixes, and suffixes and then answer the questions. Consider the literal meaning of each word.

intro –	A prefix meaning:	*in; within*
spec –	A root meaning:	*to look*
sub –	A prefix meaning:	*beneath*
post –	A prefix meaning:	*after*

1. "Spectacles" is another word for _____.

2. One who watches a sporting event is a _____.

3. To examine something or look at it very closely means that you are _____ it.

4. A period after a war is called a _____ period.

5. If you put something off until later, you _____ it.

6. Earth that is beneath the top level of soil is called _____.

7. The word "marine" refers to the sea; therefore, a boat that travels beneath the sea is a _____.

8. The literal meaning of the word "introspection" is the act of _____.

9. The stem *duc* means to lead; therefore, the literal meaning of the word "introduction" is the act of _____.

LESSON ELEVEN

Exercise I

In your own words, write a brief definition for as many words on the list as you can. Then correct and/or complete the lesson by using the mini-dictionary in the back of this book.

1. ammunition

2. anthem

3. antidote

4. assistance

5. assure

6. awkwardly

7. delightful

8. guardian

9. heartily

10. hostility

11. maneuver

12. sternly

13. suspicious

14. unusually

15. vast

Exercise II

From the list of words, fill in the blanks to make complete sentences.

1. Judge Wagner appointed a(n) _____ for the homeless children.

2. It was a(n) _____ clear day.

3. The army exercise was ended because more _____ was needed for the rifles.

4. You could almost feel the _____ between the political opponents.

5. _____, the baby took a few hesitant steps towards his father.

6. A _____ expanse of desert loomed before us.

7. "The Star Spangled Banner" is our national _____.

8. The listeners _____ agreed with the news broadcaster.

9. There was _____ available for the new exchange students.

10. The detectives watched closely as the _____ -looking woman entered the barbershop.

11. After a(n) _____ meal, we had dessert and coffee in the study.

12. Let me _____ you there will be no danger to anyone.

13. He was rushed to the hospital for a(n) _____ because he had swallowed poison.

14. With some difficulty, the man managed to _____ the piano around the tight corner.

15. Our dance instructor _____ lectured us on proper form and timing.

Exercise III

Study the following roots, prefixes, and suffixes and then answer the questions. Consider the literal meaning of each word.

vert –	A root meaning:	*to turn*
fore –	A prefix meaning:	*before; in front of*
semi –	A prefix meaning:	*half; partly; occurring twice*

1. If you revert, you _____.

2. If you turn from one religious faith to another, you are a _____.

3. An automobile with a removable roof is a _____.

4. A line that points upward is a _____ line.

5. A forewarning is a _____.

6. A country that is partly tropical is said to be a _____ country.

7. In a book, you would find the foreword at the _____.

8. The literal meaning of the word "introvert" is _____.

9. The opposite of an introvert is an extrovert. The literal meaning of "extrovert" is someone who is _____.

LESSON TWELVE

Exercise I

In your own words, write a brief definition for as many words on the list as you can. Then correct and/or complete the lesson by using the mini-dictionary in the back of this book.

1. anxiously

2. arrogantly

3. capacity

4. conversation

5. faintly

6. fierce

7. genial

8. gleaming

9. huddle

10. keenly

11. realize

12. scarce

13. secluded

14. shreds

15. suppress

Exercise II

From the list of words, fill in the blanks to make complete sentences.

1. It did not take the nurse long to _____ that the man was in great pain.

2. The girl _____ resembled her brother in appearance.

3. His _____ manner put everyone at ease.

4. The party was held in a _____ part of the beach.

5. The sick children _____ waited for their mother.

6. We became _____ aware of our mistakes as we watched the more-advanced gymnasts.

7.   There were _____ of paper all over the desk.

8.   In a _____ battle, the two stallions fought for leadership of the wild band of horses.

9.   The doctor advised him not to _____ his anger, but to deal with it.

10. The rude woman spoke _____ to the frail, old man.

11. Because of droughts, food is _____ in many parts of Africa.

12. Because of the freezing wind, we had to _____ together to stay warm.

13. It is not easy to have an intelligent _____ with a three-year old child.

14. The auditorium was filled to _____ for the opening performance.

15. The polished, silver bell was _____ in the morning sunlight.

Exercise III

Review of Roots, Prefixes, and Suffixes

1.   The word "abduct" means to kidnap; therefore, another word for "kidnapper" is _____. The person who is kidnapped is the _____.

2.   A story of a person's life is a biography. If the person writes the story of his own life, it is not a biography but an _____.

3.   If you do a job once, but then do it again, you have _____ the job.

4.   List five words with the prefix *re:*
     _____.

5.   A word that is used to indicate a female actor is _____.

6.   What can a telephoto lens on a camera do? _____

7.   The root *spec* means _____.

8.   The root *vert* means _____.

9.   The prefix *post* means _____.

10. A prefix meaning "half" or "partly" is _____.

LESSON THIRTEEN

Exercise I

In your own words, write a brief definition for as many words on the list as you can. Then correct and/or complete the lesson by using the mini-dictionary in the back of this book.

1. abolish

2. consider

3. consuming

4. convince

5. crisis

6. deserted

7. devise

8. exceed

9. gaudy

10. invade

11. nasty

12. relieved

13. reunion

14. suffocate

15. trembling

Exercise II

From the list of words, fill in the blanks to make complete sentences.

1. You should _____ all the facts before making a decision.

2. The dust blowing off the plowed field was thick enough to _____ an army of men.

3. Red Cross volunteers are available during any _____ that may occur.

4. In wartime, soldiers often _____ enemy territory.

5. The prizefighter took a _____ blow to the head.

6. I tried to _____ my parents that I was not at fault.

7.   My father said that the orange jacket looked too _____ .

8.   Our class will have its tenth _____ this year.

9.   We had to _____ a plan of attack.

10.   Please try not to _____ the speed limit.

11.   A few Southerners had hopes that they could _____ slavery without a war.

12.   An all- _____ rage came over me as I witnessed the cruel treatment of the animals.

13.   My knees were _____ because I was so frightened.

14.   The small, frightened kitten had been _____ by its owner.

15.   Minor pain can sometimes be _____ with a couple of aspirin tablets.

Exercise III

(Review - Lessons 7 – 13)
Match each word on the left to its correct definition on the right.

_____	1. admiration	A.	a dead body
_____	2. bruise	B.	physically weak; not strong
_____	3. corpse	C.	pleasure, wonder, and delight in something or someone
_____	4. dependable	D.	reliable
_____	5. frugally	E.	to live in
_____	6. inhabit	F.	a discoloration of skin caused by broken blood vessels
_____	7. frail	G.	not wastefully
_____	8. leisurely	H.	severely, grimly
_____	9. maneuver	I.	a change in course
_____	10. sternly	J.	unhurried, without haste
_____	11. shreds	K.	to hold back
_____	12. suppress	L.	small amounts; irregular strips torn from something

LESSON FOURTEEN

Exercise I

In your own words, write a brief definition for as many words on the list as you can. Then correct and/or complete the lesson by using the mini-dictionary in the back of this book.

1. accumulated

2. continue

3. curious

4. decline

5. directive

6. gentle

7. identity

8. insurmountable

9. lunge

10. penalizes

11. remedy

12. somber

13. specific

14. sympathetic

15. tangled

Exercise II

From the list of words, fill in the blanks to make complete sentences.

1. One must be _____ when handling an infant.

2. When a foul occurs in a football game, the referee _____ the offending team.

3. The boat stopped because a fish net was _____ in the propeller.

4. The principal was _____ when we explained why we were late.

5. I had to _____ his invitation to dinner because I had already eaten.

6. Bill felt his problems were _____, and he did not know where to turn for help.

7. We were given a _____ and told how to handle an emergency situation.

8. Please _____ exercising for twenty more minutes.

9. Separating the two boys on the bus did little to _____ the situation.

10. We were _____ to know who had won the million dollars.

11. Be more _____ the next time you give directions.

12. With one powerful _____, the panther jumped from the rock.

13. A _____ group of people slowly walked through the cemetery gates.

14. Because of a case of mistaken _____, the wrong person was arrested.

15. The hotel manager had already _____ over three hundred towels.

Exercise III

In addition to using words that mean the same or words that mean the opposite, another structure that analogies use Is one of function. Study the analogy below.

> *Car : garage :: airplane : _____*

A car goes in a garage just as an airplane goes in a hangar; therefore, "hangar" is the word needed to complete this analogy. Try the analogies below. We have shown various types of relationships.

1. scalpel : doctor :: magic wand : _____

2. kind : generous :: cheap : _____

3. black : white :: optimistic : _____

4. bears : cave :: occupants : _____

5. soldier : uniform :: spy: _____

6. frail : weak :: friends : _____

7. horn : warning :: baseball bat : _____

8. water : thirst :: food : _____

9. prison : criminals :: zoo : _____

LESSON FIFTEEN

Exercise I

In your own words, write a brief definition for as many words on the list as you can. Then correct and/or complete the lesson by using the mini-dictionary in the back of this book.

1. absorb

2. accompany

3. apparently

4. compensate

5. contrary

6. consumer

7. disbelieve

8. liability

9. migrant

10. mound

11. rapidly

12. rarely

13. revolver

14. slushy

15. strays

Exercise II

From the list of words, fill in the blanks to make complete sentences.

1. The streets were quite _____ as the snow melted.

2. _____ does a person get a second chance.

3. After planting the dogwood tree, there was a _____ of dirt left.

4. Some people can _____ facts more quickly than others.

5. Each September, the _____ are caught by the dogcatcher and brought to the pound.

6. During the harvest, many _____ workers find temporary jobs.

7.   It is up to the _____ to decide which products are the best buy.

8.   We were asked to _____ the younger campers to the lake.

9.   _____ to popular belief, entertainers work very hard at their jobs.

10. The game had _____ ended while we were at the concession stand.

11. The FBI agent held a loaded _____ in his hand.

12. The sun was _____ disappearing behind the tall pines as we made our way homeward.

13. The fancy computer turned out to be more of a _____ than an asset.

14. If you wish to _____ a proven theory, that's your privilege.

15. Although he worked many extra hours, his employer did not _____ Bob with either more money or time off.

Exercise III

Study the following roots, prefixes, and suffixes and then answer the questions. Consider the literal meaning of each word.

anti –	A prefix meaning:	*against*
ology –	A suffix meaning:	*the study of*
psych –	A root meaning:	*mind, soul*
pro –	A prefix meaning:	*for*
ist –	A suffix meaning:	*one who studies or believes*

1.   If you were in favor of a particular war, you might he said to be _____;

     if you were against the war, though, you would be said to be _____.

2.   The literal meaning of "psychology" is _____.

3.   The root *anthro* means man; therefore, the word "anthropology" means _____.

4.   What do you suppose "sociology" is? _____.

5.   A psychic claims to be able to read _____.

6.   A psychologist is _____

7.   A scientist is _____

8.   A behaviorist is _____

9.   Would a pro-revolutionary be for or against revolution? _____

10. An anti-Semite is someone who is_____.

LESSON SIXTEEN

Exercise I

In your own words, write a brief definition for as many words on the list as you can. Then correct and/or complete the lesson by using the mini-dictionary in the back of this book.

1.   astride

2.   commotion

3.   delicate

4.   disagreeable

5.   firm

6.   frayed

7.   frequent

8.   impolite

9.   misgivings

10. pursue

11. restrain

12. slight

13. suitable

14. shambles

15. unreasonable

Exercise II

From the list of words, fill in the blanks to make complete sentences.

1.   The family room was a _____ after my sister's slumber party.

2.   There was quite a _____ in the locker room after the ball game.

3.   Dad was in such a _____ mood that we decided not to ask for an advance on our allowance.

4.   It was with many _____ that John loaned his new car to his sister.

5.   The horse trainer sat_____ a beautiful Arabian stallion.

6. The butterfly's _____ wings fluttered in the gusty wind.

7. Less than half of high school graduates _____ a higher education.

8. Many of today's movies are not _____ for youngsters to watch.

9. In some foreign countries, it is considered _____ not to burp after eating a meal.

10. There was just a _____ difference in their ages.

11. The old sweater was _____ on the cuffs.

12. A _____ handshake is more pleasing than one that feels like a jellyfish.

13. His _____ request was not granted.

14. There are _____ thundershowers in the tropics.

15. Please try to _____ yourselves during the rock concert.

Exercise III

Study the following roots, prefixes, and suffixes and then answer the questions. Consider the literal meaning of each word.

ible, able –	A suffix meaning:	*able to; capable of*
less –	A suffix meaning:	*without*

1. If a lawn is without trees, it could be said to be _____.

2. One word which means doing something without giving any thought is _____.

3. If you drive without care, you could be accused of _____ driving.

4. A book that you can easily read may be said to be _____.

5. *Vis* means *to see;* therefore, something that is visible is _____.

6. If an object were invisible, it _____.

7. *Aud* is a root for *to hear;* therefore, something that is audible is _____.

8. What one word would indicate that something is not able to be heard? _____.

9. If you are penniless, it means that _____.

10. A person who is friendless is _____.

LESSON SEVENTEEN

Exercise I

In your own words, write a brief definition for as many words on the list as your can. Then correct and/or complete the lesson by using the mini-dictionary in the back of this book.

1. cleverly

2. dispute

3. flaw

4. gesture

5. gratefully

6. hesitate

7. midst

8. oblivious

9. obscene

10. pause

11. plead

12. resume

13. retrieve

14. scarcity

15. subdue

Exercise II

From the list of words, fill in the blanks to make complete sentences.

1. Because of the _____ of oranges, the price of juice rose.

2. In order to _____ our gear, we had to wade through deep underbrush.

3. Because of _____ calls, I had my telephone number changed.

4. The entrance into the secret passageway was _____ hidden by a full-length mirror.

5. There was quite a _____ over the referee's call.

6. After the terrible disturbance, the employees had to _____ work as if nothing had happened.

7. If you have any questions, please don't _____ to ask.

8. All donations were _____ accepted by the Salvation Army.

9. The attorney convinced his client to _____ not guilty.

10. After a short _____ for commercials, the show continued.

11. It took four police officers to _____ the drunken man.

12. I was so involved in the book, that I was _____ to the time.

13. Quite by accident, we found ourselves in the _____ of a protest march.

14. A perfect diamond is one without a _____.

15. The deputy's slight _____ with his rifle hastened the prisoner's steps.

Exercise III

Study the following roots, prefixes, and suffixes and then answer the questions. Consider the literal meaning of each word.

mater –	A root meaning:	*mother*
pater –	A root meaning:	*father*
un –	A prefix meaning:	*not, or the opposite of*

1. One word meaning not important is _____.

2. The hospital ward where a mother goes to have her child is the _____ ward.

3. Would your paternal grandparents be your mother's parents, or your father's? _____

4. One word meaning not attached is _____.

5. To lock and to bolt are words that mean somewhat the same thing. What are two other words that mean the opposite of lock and bolt? _____ and _____.

6. Another word for "tedious" or "boring" is _____.

7. Maternal instincts describe what kind of instincts? _____.

37

LESSON EIGHTEEN

Exercise I

In your own words, write a brief definition for as many words on the list as you can. Then correct and/or complete the lesson by using the mini-dictionary in the back of this book.

1. accommodate

2. adequately

3. admirer

4. aggressive

5. decade

6. endangered

7. endure

8. humiliation

9. immigrant

10. lunar

11. melancholy

12. national

13. potential

14. pretend

15. protest

Exercise II

From the list of words, fill in the blanks to make complete sentences.

1. Although the president has many _____, he also has many critics.

2. A _____ mood came over Jane as she sat looking at the rain and listening to the sad music.

3. To _____ the new grading policy, the students marched in front of the school with signs.

4. The teacher spoke to John about his _____ behavior and the way he was always pushing people around.

5. When you are young, a _____ seems like a long time, but when you are older, ten years pass very quickly.

6. It is called the "_____bird" because it represents the nation's strength.

7. The whooping crane is one of many_____ species.

8. Children often _____ to be adults when they play dress up.

9. Ingrid was a(n) _____ from Germany.

10. The warehouses were _____ stocked with provisions.

11. We were filled with _____ at our foolish error.

12. The young team had a lot of _____ but lacked experience.

13. The owners of the large farmhouse were happy to _____ the weary travelers for the evening.

14. The heat was too much to _____ for more than five minutes.

15. Tides are controlled by _____ forces.

Exercise III

Study the following roots, prefixes, and suffixes and then answer the questions. Consider the literal meaning of each word.

poly –	A prefix meaning:	*many, much*
il, in, ir –	More prefixes meaning:	*not*
port –	A root meaning:	*to carry, to move*

1. One word meaning "able to be carried" is _____.

2. Something not legal is _____.

3. Something not material is _____.

4. Something that is not regular is _____.

5. What do the following words mean?

    monogamy   _____

    bigamy   _____

    polygamy   _____

6. A geometric figure with three or more sides is a _____.

7. At a train station or airport, one who carries your baggage is a
    _____.

8. One word meaning "able to be easily moved" is _____.

LESSON NINETEEN

Exercise I

In your own words, write a brief definition for as many words on the list as you can. Then correct and/or complete the lesson by using the mini-dictionary in the back of this book.

1. agony

2. bequest

3. courteous

4. dreary

5. gloomily

6. hailed

7. haste

8. heir

9. moderate

10. resign

11. result

12. sober

13. superstition

14. unsteady

15. various

Exercise II

From the list of words, fill in the blanks to make complete sentences.

1. In my _____ to get away, I forgot my purse.

2. There are _____ ways to cook ground beef.

3. The attorney read an unusual _____ from the will.

4. With a _____ expression on his face, the sergeant read the accident report.

5. It was a _____ day, full of wind, rain, and dark clouds.

6. Prince Charles is _____ to the throne of England.

7. The belief that a black cat crossing your path brings bad luck is an unfounded _____.

8. I was in _____ before the dentist pulled my bad tooth.

9. The bellhop was not very _____ as he escorted the guests to their rooms.

10. The slaves were freed as a _____ of the Civil War.

11. We decided to _____ if we didn't get a raise this month.

12. Florida's _____ climate is very enticing to Northerners during the winter.

13. As we stood under the canopy, the doorman _____ a taxi for us.

14. The cleanup crew _____ surveyed the littered campground.

15. The horse's gait was _____ as he made his way up the rocky slope

Exercise III

Review of Roots, Prefixes and Suffixes.

1. If you were for the British, you would be said to be _____ British.
    If you were against the British, you would be said to be _____ British.

2. The root *bio* means *life*; therefore, biology is _____.

3. Do you know what the study of ancient civilizations is? _____

4. *Geo* is a root that means *earth*. What is a word for the study of the Earth? _____
    _____. A man who studies this subject is a _____.

5. The word "irreducible" means _____.

6. The suffix *less* means _____.

7. The root *mater* means _____.
    The root *pater* means _____.

8. A word that means a certain person is not able to be depended upon is _____.

9. Someone who acts too young or silly is said to be not "mature," but _____.

10. The *prefix* poly means _____.

11. The root *port* means _____.

LESSON TWENTY

Exercise I

In your own words, write a brief definition for as many words on the list as you can. Then correct and/or complete the lesson by using the mini-dictionary in the back of this book.

1. ache

2. affectionate

3. aversion

4. dazed

5. eagerly

6. expectations

7. glance

8. ignore

9. promptly

10. prosperous

11. regard

12. sheds

13. simultaneously

14. trudged

15. yelping

Exercise II

From the list of words, fill in the blanks to make complete sentences.

1. The rude man showed little _____ for the comfort of the other passengers.

2. We tried to _____ the curious stares from the crowd.

3. Every spring, a snake _____ its skin.

4. Her _____ for Jack was not hidden; soon everyone in the room knew that she could not stand him.

5. My application was _____ handled by the employment office.

6. The _____ of the dogs kept the entire neighborhood awake.

7. Jordan is a very _____ child.

8. There was a _____ look in the injured man's eyes.

9. The two leaders crossed the finish line _____, and the race was declared a tie.

10. We cannot always live up to our family's _____.

11. Because of a lack of rain, the farming community did not have a very _____ year.

12. The search party wearily _____ through the snowdrifts.

13. We are _____ awaiting summer vacation.

14. There was a dull _____ in her heart as she waved farewell.

15. A quick _____ around the room proved everything was under control.

Exercise III

(Review - Lessons 14-20)
Match each word on the left to its correct definition on the right.

_____	1.	strays	A.	to chase in order to catch
_____	2.	revolver	B.	lost animals
_____	3.	restrain	C.	offensive; indecent
_____	4.	pursue	D.	intense pain
_____	5.	obscene	E.	a pistol, gun
_____	6.	oblivious	F.	polite, considerate
_____	7.	melancholy	G.	to hold back
_____	8.	lunar	H.	a brief or hasty look
_____	9.	agony	I.	stunned or confused
_____	10.	courteous	J.	forgetful, unaware
_____	11.	dazed	K.	sad and gloomy
_____	12.	glance	L.	of, caused by, or affecting the moon

LESSON TWENTY-ONE

Exercise I

In your own words, write a brief definition for as many words on the list as you can. Then correct and/or complete the lesson by using the mini-dictionary in the back of this book.

1. anticipation

2. chuckle

3. concealed

4. cunning

5. devoted

6. evasive

7. hospitality

8. immediate

9. inevitable

10. insistent

11. resolution

12. shudder

13. situation

14. solemn

15. triumphantly

Exercise II

From the list of words, fill in the blanks to make complete sentences.

1. The hunter was as _____ as the wild animals he tracked.

2. His _____ impulse was to run away.

3. Because I never keep them, I didn't make one _____ for the new year.

4. The teacher was _____ that Martin hand her the tape player.

5. The team members put the coach on their shoulders and _____ marched off the field after their victory.

6.   The _____ of the hotel manager made us feel very welcome.

7.   Funerals are usually very_____ occasions.

8.   His _____ answers made the truant officer more suspicious.

9.   In an emergency _____, you should try to remain calm.

10. The safe was _____ behind a large portrait.

11. She _____ most of her time to practicing the violin.

12. Our _____ must have shown on our faces.

13. Knowing that his capture was _____, the fugitive surrendered.

14. There was a _____ in Santa's voice as he greeted the excited children.

15. With a _____ , the child swallowed the bitter medicine.

Exercise III

Complete the analogies.

1.   rose : flower :: revolver : _____

2.   believe : disbelieve :: credit : _____

3.   suitable : unsuitable :: met : _____

4.   plead : beg :: hesitate: _____

5.   solemn : grave :: polite: _____

6.   melancholy : sad :: guard: _____

7.   moderate : immoderate :: legal: _____

8.   gloomy : happy :: polite: _____

9.   awkward : clumsy :: walk: _____

LESSON TWENTY-TWO

Exercise I

In your own words, write a brief definition for as many words on the list as you can. Then correct and/or complete the lesson by using the mini-dictionary in the back of this book.

1. available

2. bail

3. bearings

4. exhibition

5. fatal

6. fatigue

7. instinct

8. lodging

9. novelty

10. regret

11. remote

12. snarl

13. splendid

14. tremble

15. unjustly

Exercise II

From the list of words, fill in the blanks to make complete sentences.

1. Anyone would suffer _____ after working like that for eighteen hours.

2. Because he showed no _____ for his crimes, the judge gave him a long prison sentence.

3. The travelers found _____ at a small inn on the outskirts of town.

4. My hand began to _____ as I raised the glass to my lips.

5. The teacher said that it was a _____ to ever receive homework from Joe.

6. It took quite a while to get our _____ in the blinding storm.

7. We were on a _____ island in the middle of the ocean.

8. Punishment does not have to be _____ harsh to be effective.

9. The second bullet was the _____ one that killed him.

10. After the _____ performance, the audience gave the players a standing ovation.

11. Jungle animals have an _____ for survival.

12. At the artist's first _____, many beautiful paintings were bought.

13. The only _____ tickets were too expensive.

14. With a fierce _____, the wolf leaped towards the intruder.

15. We had to _____ water out of the sinking rowboat.

Exercise III

Study the following roots, prefixes, and suffixes and then answer the questions. Consider the literal meaning of each word.

trans –	A prefix meaning:	*beyond, over, through*
circum –	A prefix meaning:	*around, surrounding*
aqua –	A root meaning:	*water*

1. To move or carry something is to _____ it.

2. If you circumnavigate the globe, you sail _____.

3. The literal meaning of circumspect is to _____.

4. An aquatic show would take place in _____.

5. A transcontinental highway _____.

6. An aquarium is filled with _____.

7. What do you suppose an aqueduct is? _____.

8. What does the word transparent mean? _____.

9. If you transmit information, what are you doing? _____.

10. If elocution refers to speaking, what does circumlocution mean? _____.

LESSON TWENTY-THREE

Exercise I

In your own words, write a brief definition for as many words on the list as you can. Then correct and/or complete the lesson by using the mini-dictionary in the back of this book.

1. boarded

2. burden

3. comforted

4. corresponded

5. crackled

6. craved

7. dreadful

8. grieving

9. heal

10. infiltrating

11. nipped

12. puzzled

13. regained

14. stranded

15. threatened

Exercise II

From the list of words, fill in the blanks to make complete sentences.

1. It was a _____ blow to his ego to lose the competition.

2. A warm fire _____ cheerfully in the den.

3. Most minor wounds _____ in a few days.

4. When his father finally returned home, it was as if a tremendous _____ had been lifted from his shoulders.

5. The _____ widow left the church alone.

6. All of the returning veterans _____ a home-cooked meal.

7. Although we closed all the windows, the smoke was still _____ our house.

8. The playful puppy _____ at the child's ankle.

9. We were left _____ in the desert after the thief stole our jeep.

10. We were all _____; not one of us knew the answer.

11. I haven't _____ with Aunt Grace for several months.

12. The clown almost fell off the wire, but he _____ his balance at the last moment.

13. Last minute passengers _____ the overloaded plane.

14. The girl _____ to tell the principal if John did not give back her ring.

15. She _____ the lost child until his mother returned.

Exercise III

Study the following roots, prefixes, and suffixes and then answer the questions. Consider the literal meaning of each word.

cide –	A root meaning:	*to kill*
counter –	A prefix meaning:	*against*
ism –	A suffix meaning:	*a belief in*

1. The root *sui* means *self*; therefore, suicide means _____

2. What is patricide? _____

3. *Reg* is a root meaning king. What is the word that describes the killing of a king?
    _____

4. If you travel in a counterclockwise direction, what direction are you going?
    _____

5. If a general countermands an order of a captain, what has he done? _____
    _____

6. When you move to counteract an opponent, what are you doing? _____
    _____

7. An insecticide is a something that is used to _____.

8. Study the word "counterterrorism." What do you think it means? _____
    _____

9. *Pax* or *pac* is a root meaning peace. What do you suppose pacifism is? _____

LESSON TWENTY-FOUR

Exercise I

In your own words, write a brief definition for as many words on the list as you can. Then correct and/or complete the lesson by using the mini-dictionary in the back of this book.

1. abandoned

2. alleged

3. depressing

4. despised

5. discontented

6. dismissed

7. engulfed

8. horrified

9. lopsided

10. mutilated

11. publicized

12. refrained

13. shivering

14. staggering

15. tingled

Exercise II

From the list of words, fill in the blanks to make complete sentences.

1. In minutes the old, wooden building was _____ in flames.

2. The unhappy, _____ students staged a protest outside the school.

3. Although the movie was _____ on the radio and television, I had never heard of it.

4. Whoever _____ the stray cats was very cruel and should be arrested.

5. Because I sat with my foot under me for too long, it _____ when I stood up.

50

6. The load on the truck was so _____ that I was afraid that the truck would tip over.

7. "You are not _____ until the bell rings," the teacher shouted.

8. A _____ blow sent the boxer to the floor.

9. It was a very _____ day; I lost my job, and my good friend died.

10. He was standing in the snow, _____ from the cold.

11. He _____ from telling about my involvement. I was really surprised because I was sure that he would talk to save his own skin.

12. The sailors _____ the ship when it caught fire and started to sink.

13. She had a _____ look on her face when she saw the large snake.

14. Everyone knew that I _____ him, but I would not kill him.

15. It is only _____ that I stole it, so don't call me a crook.

Exercise III

Study the following roots, prefixes, and suffixes and then answer the questions. Consider the literal meaning of each word.

extra –	A prefix meaning:	*outside; beyond; more than*
mort –	A root meaning:	*death*
theo –	A root meaning:	*god; religion*

1. An extracurricular activity is an activity that is _____.

2. *Ter* is a root meaning *earth;* therefore, an extraterrestrial creature is something _____ _____.

3. Sensory refers to our five senses: touch, taste, sight, smell, and hearing; therefore, extrasensory experiences must refer to _____.

4. In a mortuary, you probably would find _____.

5. A mortician is _____.

6. When we recognize our own mortality, we recognize that someday everyone _____ _____.

7. If God is immortal, it means that _____.

8. Theology is _____ .

9. The prefix *a* means *not;* therefore an atheist is _____ and atheism _____ .

10. Monotheism is the _____ and polytheism is _____.

51

LESSON TWENTY-FIVE

Exercise I

In your own words, write a brief definition for as many words on the list as you can. Then correct and/or complete the lesson by using the mini-dictionary in the back of this book.

1. bulky

2. drooped

3. fraud

4. immune

5. impulse

6. nutrient

7. optimistic

8. pace

9. peeped

10. predicament

11. prohibit

12. survivors

13. unfortunately

14. visible

15. waged

Exercise II

From the list of words, fill in the blanks to make complete sentences.

1. Megan's shoulders _____ noticeably after she was turned down for the new job.

2. On a(n) _____, I decided to buy a new Corvette.

3. One of the _____ of the shipwreck was picked up by helicopter.

4. Halley's comet was not _____ to the naked eye.

5. The load was _____, but not too heavy to handle.

6. Income tax _____ is punishable by imprisonment and/or fine or both.

7. We were not able to finish the job on time, _____ .

8. There are laws to _____ the sale of alcohol to minors.

9. Vitamin C is a necessary _____ in a balanced diet.

10. At Gettysburg, a fierce battle was _____ .

11. The brisk _____ of the seasoned hikers was hard to match.

12. You should be _____ about the future, not pessimistic.

13. We were in quite a(n) _____ after losing the car keys.

14. I am not _____ to the measles, nor are you.

15. A few rays of sunshine _____ from under the clouds.

Exercise III

Study the following roots, prefixes, and suffixes and then answer the questions. Consider the literal meaning of each word.

vok, voc –	A root meaning:	*voice, call*
super –	A prefix meaning:	*more than*
ward –	A suffix meaning:	*in the direction of*

1. A vocal arrangement is a musical arrangement made to _____.

2. Someone who is vociferous is likely to be _____.

3. If your license is revoked _____.

4. If you provoke someone, you _____.

5. Something that is superior is _____.

6. If you speak in superlatives about someone, you are _____.

7. Literally, a supermarket means _____.

8. The literal meaning of "supersonic" is _____.

9. If we turn homeward, we have _____.

10. If we look heavenward, we look _____.

LESSON TWENTY-SIX

Exercise I

In your own words, write a brief definition for as many words on the list as you can. Then correct and/or complete the lesson by using the mini-dictionary in the back of this book.

1. abort

2. abundant

3. alien

4. banish

5. clenches

6. dispose

7. enlarge

8. flawless

9. harass

10. juvenile

11. mangle

12. obscure

13. quench

14. renegades

15. scheme

Exercise II

From the list of words, fill in the blanks to make complete sentences.

1. The border patrol stopped his car and accused him of being an illegal _____.

2. When the baby _____ his teeth, I cannot put the spoon in his mouth.

3. The soldiers were chasing three _____ who had participated in attacks on the fort.

4. Math may seem _____ to you, but that means you have to work much harder to understand it.

5. If you continue to _____ the other students on the bus, you will be walking to school.

6. Be careful! If you catch your sleeve in that machine, it will _____ your arm.

7. The police caught him trying to _____ of the body.

8. Soda does not _____ your thirst as well as water does.

9. As the plane touched down on the runway the pilot suddenly had to _____ the landing because a truck drove out on the airstrip.

10. If you would care to _____ upon your answer, we shall await your words.

11. He said that this time he had a _____ to win at the racetrack, but as usual he lost his whole paycheck.

12. The girls thought that boys their own age were _____, but their mother would not permit them to go out with older boys.

13. He thought his plan to rob the bank was _____, but he was caught and arrested within twenty-four hours.

14. Because of his behavior, the rest of the members voted to _____ him from the club.

15. Although there was _____ food in the city, people were not eating because they could not afford to pay the prices.

Exercise III

Study the following roots, prefixes, and suffixes and then answer the questions. Consider the literal meaning of each word.

cred –	A root word meaning:	*belief, trust*
dis –	A prefix meaning:	*the negation or lack of*
ped –	A root word meaning:	*foot, feet*

1. If you show a lack of respect for someone, you have showed _____.

2. Remember that *ible* means able to; then "credible" means something that is _____ _____.

3. Something that is incredible is, therefore, _____.

4. If you give credit to someone, you are giving _____.

5. What does it mean if a story is discredited? _____

6. Define the word "pedal." _____

7. A pedestrian is one who does what? _____

8. A manicurist is someone who cuts and treats your fingernails. What do you suppose a pedicure is? _____

9. A pedestrian walkway or bridge is where _____ .

LESSON TWENTY-SEVEN

Exercise I

In your own words, write a brief definition for as many words on the list as you can. Then correct and/or complete the lesson by using the mini-dictionary in the back of this book.

1. abrupt

2. abuse

3. appropriate

4. barrier

5. collapse

6. ebony

7. exclusion

8. gait

9. hazardous

10. irrational

11. liberal

12. maze

13. paramount

14. random

15. reptiles

Exercise II

From the list of words, fill in the blanks to make complete sentences.

1. Some people think that _____ are slimy, but they are not.

2. The overturned chemical truck created a _____ situation, so the school was evac- uated.

3. Following the _____ of the tiny nation's government, many of the ethnic groups began to fight with each other.

4. Slow down gradually when you see a red light; do not race up to it and make an _____ stop.

5. The white and _____ box had figures drawn on it.

6. He did poorly on the last test, so he hoped the teacher was a _____ grader.

7. The little girl sitting on her porch was hit by a shot fired at _____ by a man police said could give no reason for his actions.

8. If you continue to _____ the equipment, you're off the team.

9. The _____ of Johnson's name from the program was accidental, and not done on purpose.

10. He knew that whistling during the assembly was not _____ behavior, so he must now expect to be punished.

11. The _____ at which she walked was too fast for me to keep up.

12. When he becomes _____, it is best to leave the area because you know he is going to get into trouble.

13. "The only _____ to your success," my father said, "is yourself."

14. _____ to success is getting a good education in whatever field of work you choose.

15. The dark, narrow streets, which frequently ended in dead ends, seemed such a _____ that he began to feel he would never get out of the city.

Exercise III

Study the following roots, prefixes, and suffixes and then answer the questions. Consider the literal meaning of each word.

re –	A prefix meaning:	*again*
init –	A root meaning:	*beginning, first*
micro –	A root meaning:	*small*

1. If you had to restart a car, you would have to _____.

2. Your initials are _____.

3. If you failed in your initial attempt but succeeded on your second try, your initial attempt was your _____.

4. People who are initiated into a club are _____ members.

5. If you initial a report, you are putting down your _____. If you re-initial it, you are _____.

6. A microscope is used to look at _____ organisms.

7. The reason a spy would put secrets on microfilm is _____.

8. Meter means to measure; therefore, a micrometer must be used to measure _____
_____.

LESSON TWENTY-EIGHT

Exercise I

In your own words, write a brief definition for as many words on the list as you can. Then correct and/or complete the lesson by using the mini-dictionary in the back of this book.

1. abstain

2. accusation

3. authentic

4. chunk

5. cosmetics

6. elevate

7. fidget

8. genocide

9. hinder

10. jest

11. luxury

12. meddle

13. paternal

14. rave

15. retain

Exercise II

From the list of words, fill in the blanks to make complete sentences.

1. It was a replica, not an _____ Civil War uniform.

2. The girl, although a natural beauty, spent most of her money on _____ because she felt she was not pretty enough.

3. Sit still; when you _____, it makes you look guilty.

4. The comment was made in _____; I didn't really mean that you lied to me.

5. Take care of your own business, and you won't have time to _____ in your neighbor's.

6. Our team could not _____ control of the ball; that is why we lost the game.

7. If you put a _____ of ice in the cooler, it will keep the sodas cold.

8. Although he was innocent, he knew that the mere _____ could hurt his reputation in the town.

9. In that situation, you should _____ his feet so they are higher than his head.

10. If I get home late, my father will _____ for hours, so it is easier to be home on time.

11. I guess my father did not have much of a _____ instinct since he rarely bothered to see me.

12. It is of paramount importance, if you are to be successful, to _____ from drugs and alcohol.

13. Those Nazi war criminals were tried for _____, because they were responsible for attempting to wipe out whole groups of people.

14. As a young girl from a family who could barely provide the necessities in life, she was determined to become successful so her children might have some _____ in life.

15. Know what you want, work hard to get it, and do not let others _____ you.

Exercise III

Study the following roots, prefixes, and suffixes and then answer the questions. Consider the literal meaning of each word.

scribe, script –	A root meaning:	*to write*
ship –	A suffix meaning:	*the art of, or skill of*
en –	A suffix meaning:	*to make*

1. If you say a person has shown great seamanship, what is it you have said?
   _____

2. If you wished to say that Tommy made a fence post weaker when he hit it with his car, you might say he _____ it.

3. What have you done if you lessen the amount called for in a recipe? _____

4. If you make something brighter, you have _____ it.

5. If you take something that is loose and tighten it, you have _____ it.

6. If you inscribe your initials on a ring, you have _____.

7. Literally, "Holy Scripture" is _____.

8. *Manu* means *hand*, so literally a manuscript must be _____.

9. If you sent for a transcript of a television news show, you would receive a _____
   _____.

MINI -DICTIONARY

NOTE: For many words, you will be able to find the exact form you are seeking. With a few though, you will only find a variation of the word.
Example: *"snug" instead of "snugly"; " publicize" instead of "publicized"*

pronunciation key

ă	hat, final, menace	ô	order
ā	age, face, rate, acorn	oi	oil, voice
ä	father, far	ōō	moon
		ou	house, out
b	bad, rob		
ch	child, much	p	paper, cup
d	did, red	r	run, try
		s	say, yes
ĕ	let, best, tend	sh	she, rush
ē	equal, be, eve	t	tell, it
er	term, learn	th	thin, both
		th	then, smooth
f	fat, if		
g	go, bag	ŭ	full, put
h	he, how	ü	rule, move
		ū	use, music
ĭ	it, pin, city		
ī	ice, five, pine	v	very, save
		w	will, woman
j	jam, enjoy, gentle	y	young, yet
k	kind, seek	z	zero, breeze
l	land, coal	zh	measure, seizure
m	me, am		
n	no, in	ə	represents:
ng	long, bring		a about
			e taken
ŏ	hot, rock, dog		i April
ō	open, go, note		o lemon
			u circus

60

abandoned (ə băn´ dənd) deserted; gave up; stopped trying

abolish (ə bŏl´ ĭsh) to put an end to; to do away with

abort (a bôrt´) to end before natural completion

abrupt (ə brŭpt´) unexpected, sudden; short and brief

absorb (ăb sôrb´) to take in; soak up

abstain (ăb stān) to voluntarily keep from doing something

abundant (ə bŭn´ dənt) very plentiful; in great supply

abuse (ə byōōz´) to use improperly; to hurt or injure by treating badly

accident (ăk´ sə dənt) something that happens without being planned in advance

accommodate (ə kŏm´ ə dāt) to provide with lodging; to do a favor

accompany (ə kŭm´ pə nē) to go along with

accomplishment (ə kŏm´ plĭsh mənt) an achievement; something done successfully

accumulate (ə kū´ myə lāt) to collect or to pile up

accurate (ăk´ yə rĭt) correct; right

accusation (ăk yōō zā´ shən) a statement that a person is guilty of a wrong- doing

ache (āk) a steady pain

acquaintance (ə kwānt´ ns) person who one knows; a friend

adequate (ăd´ ə kwĭt) sufficient, suitable; acceptable

admiration (ăd´ mə rā´ shən) respect

admire (ăd mīr´) to feel respect or love for another

adoration (ăd ə rā´ shən) great and devoted love

affectionate (ə fĕk´ shən ĭt) tender, loving

aggressive (ə grĕs´ ĭv) quick to attack or to start a fight; bold; forward

agony (ăg´ ə nē) intense and prolonged pain or suffering

alien (ā´ lē ən) coming from another country

allege (ə lĕj´) to state as true, but not prove

ammunition (ăm´ yĕ nĭsh´ ən) anything that can be shot from a weapon

ancient (ān´ shənt) very old

annual (ăn´ yōō əl) yearly; once a year

anthem (ăn´ thəm) a song of praise or loyalty

anticipation (ăn tĭs´ ə pā´ shən) expectation; eagerly awaiting

antidote (ăn´ tə dōt) a remedy to counteract a poison

anxiously (ăngk´ shəs lē) worriedly; uneasily

apparently (ə păr´ ənt lē) obviously; easily understood

appropriate (ə prō´ prē ĭt) suitable for a particular person, occasion, or place

armored (är´ mərd) covered with heavy metal

arrogant (ăr´ ə gənt) in a self-important manner; smug

assistance (ə sĭst´ ns) help; aid

assure (ə shür´) to declare confidently; to make certain

astonishing (əs tŏn´ ĭsh ĭng) amazing, surprising

astride (ə strīd´) with a leg on each side of

authentic (ô thĕn´ tĭk) true, credible; not counterfeit or copied

avail (ə vāl´) capable of being obtained; able to be gotten

aversion (ə vĕr´ zhən) an intense dislike; a turning away from

awkwardly (ôk´ wərd lē) clumsily

bail (bāl) to remove water by repeatedly filling a container and emptying it

banish (băn´ ĭsh) to force someone to leave a country or place; to drive away

bare (bār) to expose

barrier (băr´ ē ər) a fence, wall, or other structure that blocks off a passageway

bearing (bār´ ĭng)   whereabouts; direction

bequest (bĭ kwēst´)   something given in a will

blunder (blŭn´ dər)   to act clumsily or stupidly

boarded (bôrd´ ĭd)   went into or on a bus, train, plane, etc.

brilliant (brĭl´ yənt)   vivid; shining brightly

bruise (brüz)   discoloration of skin caused from broken blood vessels

bulky (bŭl´ kē)   taking up much space

burden (bërd´ n)   a great weight; a heavy load

capacity (kə păs´ ə tē)   the ability to hold or contain; maximum amount

caution (kô´ shən)   care so as to avoid trouble or danger

cautious (kô´ shəs)   careful

chuckle (chŭk´ l)   a quiet laugh

chunk (chŭngk)   a thick piece of something

clench (klĕnch)   to close one's hands or teeth tightly

clever (klĕv´ ər)   intelligent or smart

cliff (klĭf)   a high, steep rock

clutch (klŭch)   hold tightly

collapse (kə lăps´)   to fall suddenly

comfort (kŭm´ fərt)   to soothe; to calm down; to aid

commotion (kə mō´ shən)   disturbance; a loud uproar

compensate (kŏm´ pən sāt)   to make up for; to pay for work or damages

conceal (kən sēl´)   to hide

confirm (kən fërm´)   to make something definite or binding

consider (kən sĭd´ ər)   to think over

consult (kən sŭlt´)   to go to for advice; to talk things over

consume (kən süm´)   to overwhelm or overpower; to use goods; to eat

consumer (kən sōō´ ər)   someone who buys and uses goods

contented (kən tĕn´ tid)   satisfied

continue (kən tĭn´ ū)   to keep on or persist

contrary (kŏn´ trĕr ē)   completely different; the opposite of

conversation (kŏn vər sā´ shən)   an informal talk; discussion

convince (kən vĭns´)   to persuade; to overcome one's doubts

coroner (kôr´ ə nər)   an official who investigates the causes of a death

corpse (kôrps)   a dead body, usually human

correspond (kôr´ ə spŏnd)   to communicate by letter; to write

cosmetics (kŏz mĕt´ ĭks)   preparations such as face powder or skin cream

courteous (kër´ tē əs)   polite; considerate

crackle (krăk´ l)   to make sharp, snapping sounds

crate (krāt)   a packing case made of slats of wood

crave (krāv)   to have a strong desire for

craze (krāz)   to be mad or insane

crisis (krī´ sĭs)   a time of danger; a decisive; crucial point

critical (krĭt´ ə kl)   likely to find fault

cunning (kŭn´ ĭng)   sly, crafty, clever

curator (kyü rā´ tər)   a person in charge of a museum, library, or zoo

curious (kyür´ ē əs)   eager to acquire knowledge; unusual

daze (dāz)   to stun or confuse

decade (dĕk´ ād)   ten years

decline (dĭ klīn´)   to refuse; to turn down

defective (dĭ fĕk´ tĭv)   faulty; not working properly

delicate (dĕl´ ə kĭt)   easily broken or damaged; fragile

delightful (dĭ līt´ fəl)   very pleasing

denial (dĭ nī´ əl)   declaring something to be untrue

depart (dĭ pärt´)   to go away, leave

depend (dĭ pĕnd´)   to rely on; to trust

depress (dǐ prĕs´) to be gloomy or sad

desert (dǐ zërt´) to abandon; to leave alone

despise (dǐ spīz´) to regard with contempt or scorn; to dislike intensely

deteriorate (dǐ tër´ ə rāt) to break down in quality or value

devise (dǐ vīz´) to plan, invent

devoted (dǐ vōt´ id) dedicated; very loyal

direct (də rǐkt´) to order; to instruct

disagreeable (dǐs ə grē´ ə bl) unpleasant; offensive

disaster (də zǎs´ tər) great destruction or misfortune

disbelieve (dǐs bǐ lēv´) to refuse to believe in; to reject

discard (dǐs kärd´) to throw away

discontented (dǐs kən tĕn´ tǐd) not satisfied; uneasy

discussion (dǐs kush´ ən) conversation; informal talk

disguise (dǐs gīz´) to conceal or to cover up

disgust (dǐs gŭst´) an annoying or very disagreeable feeling

dismal (dǐz´ ml) dreary

dismiss (dǐs mǐs´) to discharge; allow to leave

dispose (dǐ spōz´) to get rid of; throw out

dispute (dǐs pūt´) an argument or disagreement

domesticate (də mĕs´ tə kāt) to make tame

dreadful (drĕd´ fəl) terrible; inspiring great fear

dreary (drǐr´ ē) gloomy; dismal; depressing

droop (drōōp) to bend or hang downward; sag

eager (ē´ gər) enthusiastic or impatient

eavesdropper (ēvz´ drŏp´ ər) one who listens secretly to a private conversation

ebony (ĕb´ ə nē) a hard, black wood

edible (ĕd´ ə bl) fit to eat; able to be eaten

efficient (ə fǐsh´ ənt) producing effectively with a minimum of waste or effort

elevate (ĕl ə vāt´) to raise to a higher position; to lift up

embarrassment (ĕm bǎr´ əs mənt) the condition of feeling ill at ease

emerge (ǐ mërj´) to come into view; appear

endanger (ĕn dān´ jər) to place in danger; to expose to loss

endure (ĕn dür´ or ĕn dyür´) put up with

engulf (ĕn gŭlf´) to enclose; to swallow up

enlarge (ĕn lärj´) to make larger

entries (ĕn´ trēz) listed items, as in a diary or register

entry (ĕn´ trē) entrance or passage

evacuate (ǐ vǎk´ yü āt) to withdraw or depart from

evade (ǐ vād´) to avoid doing or answering directly

exact (ǐg zǎkt´) precise in detail; completely correct

exceed (ek sēd´) to be greater than; to surpass

excess (ĕk sĕs´ or ĕk´ sĕs) more than what is normal or sufficient

exclusion (ǐk sklōō´ zhən) the act of keeping someone out of a place, group, or activity

exhibition (ĕk sə bǐsh´ ən) a display for the public

expectation (ĕks´ pĕk tā´ shən) prospect; hope

extensive (ĕks tĕn´ sǐv) large in area or amount; vast

extinct (ĕks tingkt´) no longer existing in living form

extreme (ĕks trēm´) very great or intense

faint (fānt) not clear; slight

fasten (fǎs´ n) join; connect

fatal (fā´ tl) causing death; disastrous

fate (fāt) what will happen or has happened to a person

fatigue (fə tēg´) weariness or exhaustion resulting from hard work or strain

feverish (fē´ vər ĭsh) in an agitated state, intensely emotional

fidget (fĭj´ ĭt) to move uneasily or nervously

fierce (fērs) wild and savage; ferocious

firm (fĕrm) strong and sure; steady, not changing

flaw (flô) a blemish or defect

flawless (flô´ lĭs) without a mistake, perfect

flush (flŭsh) to turn red in the face; blush

formidable (fôr´ mə də bl) inspiring fear, dread, or alarm

frail (frāl) physically weak; not strong

fraud (frôd) a deliberate deception; a swindle

fray (frā) to unravel; to make ragged

frequent (frē´ kwənt) occurring at close intervals; often

frugal (frü´ gl) not wasteful; cheap

gait (gāt) a way of walking or running

gaudy (gôd´ ē) too showy to be in good taste

genial (jēn´ yəl) cheerful, friendly, and good-humored

genocide (jĕn´ ə sīd) the deliberate wiping out or killing off of a racial or cultural group

gentle (jĕn´ tl) kind, tender, or soothing

gesture (jĕs´ chər) a motion of hands, arms, or body to help express meaning

glance (glăns) a brief or hasty look

gleam (glēm) to shine brightly

glitter (glĭt´ ər) to sparkle brilliantly

gloomily (glü´ mə lē) dismally or drearily; sadly

glow (glō) shine with warm color

grateful (grāt´ fəl) thankful

grief (grēf) intense sorrow

grieve (grēv) to feel deep sorrow

guardian (gär´ dē ən) someone who protects, defends, or takes care of another

hail (hāl) signal in order to get the attention of

hamper (hăm´ pər) to prevent the progress or action of

harass (hăr´ əs) to bother or torment another

harness (här´ nĭs) to bring under control and direct the force of

harsh (härsh) unpleasant; extremely severe

haste (hāst) swiftness of motion or action; quick, hurried

hasten (hās´ n) to hurry; go quickly

hazardous (hăz´ ər dəs) dangerous

heal (hēl) to make healthy

heartily (här´ tə lē) in a warm and friendly manner

heir (ār) a person who inherits or is entitled to inherit property, etc.

hesitate (hĕz´ ə tāt) to pause or waver; to delay in acting or choosing

hideous (hĭd´ ē əs) horribly ugly

hinder (hĭn´ dər) to interfere with or prevent action or progress

horrify (hôr´ ə fī) to shock

hospitality (hŏs pə tăl´ ə tē) the act of being friendly to guests

hostility (hŏs tĭl´ ə tē) unfriendliness; anger; hatred

huddle (hŭd´ l) to crowd together

humiliation (hū mĭl ē ā´ shən) disgrace or embarrassment

identical (ĭ dĕn´ tə kl) exactly alike

identity (ĭ dĕn´ tə tē) being recognized as a certain person or thing

ignore (ĭg nôr´) to pay no attention to; to disregard

illustrate (ĭl´ əs trāt) to make clear or explain by using examples or pictures

imagination (ĭ măj´ ə nā´ shən) the act of creating images of something not present

imitation (ĭm´ ə tā shən) something copied from or patterned after another

immediate (ĭ mē´ dē ĭt) taking place at once; without delay

immigrant (ĭm´ ə grənt) one who is a new arrival in a country

immobilize (ĭm mō´ blīz) to make incapable of movement; to keep in place

immune (ĭ mün´) protected; safe from something

impolite (ĭm´ pə līt) discourteous, unmannerly; not polite

impulse (ĭm´ pŭls) a sudden urge or whim

incredible (ĭn krĕd´ ə bl) unbelievable; not able to be believed

inevitable (ĭn ĕv´ ə tə bl) not capable of being avoided or prevented

inexpensive (ĭn ĕks pĕn´ sĭv) low-priced; cheap

infiltrating (ĭn fĭl´ trāt ĭng) entering something

inhabit (ĭn hăb´ ĭt) to live in

initial (ĭ nĭsh´ əl) first; beginning

injurious (ĭn jŭr´ ē əs) likely to cause injury; harmful, damaging

insistent (ĭn sĭs´ tənt) firm in stating a demand or opinion

instinct (ĭn´ stĭngkt) a natural talent or ability; not learned behavior

insurmountable (ĭn sər mount´ əbl) cannot be overcome

intent (ĭn tĕnt´) to have the mind fixed on something

intercept (ĭn´ tər sept´) to stop the progress of something

international (ĭn´ tər năsh´ ən l) between two or more nations

invade (ĭn vād´) to enter in order to attack; overrun

irrational (ĭ răsh´ ə nəl) not capable of thinking clearly

irrigation (ĭr ə gā´ shən) supplied with water by means of streams or pipes

irritable (ĭr´ ə tə bl) easily annoyed

item (ĭ´ təm) a single unit; a piece of news

jest (jĕst) something said or done for fun

juvenile (jōō´ və nəl) young, immature, childish

keen (kēn) piercing, sharp

late (lāt) recently deceased, dead

legitimate (lə jĭt´ ə mĭt) legal; reasonable; authentic

leisurely (lē´ zhər lē) without haste or exertion; unhurried

liability (lī´ ə bĭl ə tē) something that holds one back

liberal (lĭb´ ər əl) tending to give generously

lodging (lŏj´ ĭng) a temporary place to sleep

lopsided (lŏp sīd´ ĭd) higher on one side than the other

lunar (lü´ nər) of, caused by, or affecting the moon

lunge (lŭnj) a sudden, forceful movement forward

magnificent (măg nĭf´ ə snt) splendid in appearance

maneuver (mə nü´ vər) a change in course

mangle (mĕng´ gəl) to disfigure by crushing; to ruin

materialize (mə tĭr´ ē əl īz) to become real; to appear from nowhere

maze (māz) a confusing network of pathways

meddle (mĕd´ l) to interfere in another's business

melancholy (mĕl´ ən kŏl ē) sad and gloomy

menace (mĕn´ ĭs) threat of harm; danger

midst (mĭdst) being among members of a group

migrant (mī´ grənt) one who moves from one area to another

miserable (mĭz´ ər ə bl) very unhappy

misgiving (mĭs gĭv´ ĭng) feeling of doubt or concern

moderate (mŏd´ ər ĭt) not excessive or extreme; mild, calm

65

mound (mound) a pile or mass of anything; a small hill

mutilate (mū´ tl āt) to damage, to destroy a necessary part

mutual (mū´ chü əl) done or felt by two; shared in common

mysterious (mĭs tĭr´ ē əs) difficult or impossible to understand or explain

narrate (nă rāt´) to recite; to tell

nasty (năs´ tē) filthy and disgusting

national (năsh´ ən l) maintained or supported by the government of a country

navigate (năv´ ə gāt) to pilot and control the course of something

neglect (nĭ glĕkt´) to ignore; not to care for

nip (nĭp) to give small, sharp bites to

novelty (nŏv´ l tē) refreshingly new; different

nuisance (nü´ sns or nū´ sns) an annoyance or bother

numb (nŭm) without power to feel or move normally

nutrient (nū´ trĭ ənt) something that nourishes

oblivious (əb lĭv´ ē əs) preoccupied, forgetful; unaware or unmindful

obscene (ŏb´ sēn) offensive to decency; lewd; disgusting

obscure (əb skyŏōr´) vague; difficult to understand

occupant (ŏk´ yə pənt) a person dwelling or living in a place

occupy (ŏk´ yə pī) to dwell in; to live in

odor (ō´ dər) scent; smell

opponent (ə pō´ nənt) a person who opposes another; a foe

optimistic (ŏp tə mĭs´ tĭk) showing hope

pace (pās) a step made in walking; a stride

panic (păn´ ĭk) sudden and overwhelming terror

paramount (păr´ ə mount´) first in rank or importance

partially (pär´ shəl ē) not completely

paternal (pə tûr´ nəl) of a father, fatherly

pause (pôz) a brief stop; a hesitation

peep (pēp) to look out from a concealed place

penalize (pē´ nə lĭz´) to punish for an offense

persistent (pər sĭs´ tənt) refusing to give up or let go

personnel (pūr´ sə nĕl´) people employed

pessimistic (pĕs´ ə mĭs´ tĭk) expecting the worst; having little hope

petty (pĕt´ ē) small or trivial; spiteful, mean

picturesque (pĭk´ chər ĕsk´) like a picture

plantation (plăn tā´ shən) a large farm with live-in workers

plead (plēd) to appeal or beg

plunge (plŭnj) to throw or rush into

possibility (pŏs´ ə bĭl´ ə tē) something that may happen

potential (pə tĕn´ shəl) possible, but not definite, in the future

predicament (prĭ dĭk´ ə mənt) a difficult situation

prediction (prĭ dĭk´ shən) something told in advance

pretend (prĭ tĕnd´) to make believe

produce (prŏd´ ōōs) farm products, such as fruits or vegetables

prohibit (prō hĭb´ ĭt) to prevent by law or authority; forbid

prompt (prŏmpt) quick, immediate

prosperous (prŏs´ pər əs) vigorous and healthy; successful; rich

protest (prə tĕst´) to object

publicize (pŭb´ lĭ sīz´) to advertise; to give publicity to

pursue (pər sōō´) to chase in order to catch

pursuit (pər sōōt´) the act of chasing in order to capture or kill

puzzle (pŭz´l) to confuse; to mix up

quench (kwĕnch) to satisfy a thirst

rage (rāj) a great force, violence

random (răn´dəm) having no particular pattern or purpose

ransom (răn´səm) payment made to obtain release

rapid (răp´ĭd) swift, quick

rarely (rār´lē) seldom, infrequently, not often

rave (rāv) to speak in a wild way without making any sense

realize (rē´əl īz) to be fully aware; to understand fully

refrain (rĭ frān´) to hold back, restrain

refreshing (rĭ frĕsh´ĭng) different in a pleasant way

regain (rĭ gān´) recover, get back

regard (rĭ gärd´) to consider in a particular way; respect

regret (rĭ grĕt´) to feel sorry about

relief (rĭ lēf´) ease from pain, discomfort, or anxiety

relieve (rĭ lēv´) to free from pain, discomfort, or anxiety

reluctant (rĭ luk´tənt) unwilling

remedy (rĕm´ə dē) something that corrects a fault; a medicine

remote (rĭ mōt´) located far away; isolated

renegade (rĕn´ĭ gād´) a deserter, a traitor

reptiles (rĕp´tīls) cold blooded animals, such as snakes or turtles

resemble (rĭ zĕm´bl) to be alike; similar in appearance

resident (rĕz´ə dənt) one who lives in a particular place

resign (rĭ zīn´) to give up or quit

resolution (rĕz ə lü´shən) a vow or pledge

restrain (rĭ strān´) to hold back

result (rĭ zŭlt´) outcome

resume (rĭ züm´) to begin again; to continue

retain (rĭ tān´) to keep possession of

retreat (rĭ trēt´) to fall back or withdraw

retrieve (rĭ trēv´) to get back or recover

reunion (rē ūn´yən) a gathering after a separation

revenge (rĭ vĕnj´) punishment in return for an injury or insult

revolver (rĭ vŏl´vĕr) a pistol

sap (săp) to deplete or weaken gradually

savage (săv´ĭj) untouched by civilization; wild

scarce (skârs) insufficient to meet requirements; in short supply

scarcity (skâr´sə tē) a shortage

scheme (skēm) a plan for doing something

secluded (sĭ klüd´ĭd) isolated, remote

senseless (sĕns´lĭs) unconscious; lacking good judgment

serious (sĭr´ē əs) grave, sober; not joking

shambles (shăm´blz) a scene of great disorder or destruction

shed (shĕd) to lose or cast off by natural process

shiver (shĭv´ər) to shake or tremble from fear or cold

shred (shrĕd) small amount; irregular strip torn from something

shrill (shrĭl) high-pitched and piercing sound

shudder (shŭd´ər) to tremble or shiver suddenly or convulsively

sight (sīt) observation; something seen

simulate (sĭm´yōō lāt´) imitate; pretend interest

simultaneous (sī´ml tā´nē əs) at the same time

situation (sĭch´ü ā´shən) a person's position with respect to conditions

slight (slīt) small in amount or degree

slush (slŭsh) partly melted snow

snarl (snärl) an angry or threatening growl

snug (snŭg) cozy, comfortable

soar (sôr) to rise or fly high into the air

sober (sō´ bər) serious or grave; not happy

solemn (sŏl´ əm) serious, gloomy

somber (sŏm´ bər) melancholy, dismal

soothe (süth) to relieve or comfort

specific (spĭ sĭf´ ĭk) definite; limiting or limited

splendid (splĕn´ did) excellent in quality or achievement; magnificent

stagger (stăg´ ər) to move unsteadily

standard (stăn´ dərd) average, typical

stern (stĕrn) severe, grim; strict

strand (strănd) to leave in a difficult or helpless position

stray (strā) lost animal

stricken (strĭk´ ən) afflicted, wounded

subdue (səb dū´) to quiet or bring under control; to overcome

suffocate (sŭf´ ə kāt) to choke, smother

suitable (süt´ ə bl) appropriate; proper

superstition (sü´ pər stish´ ən) a belief without logical explanation

suppress (sə prĕs´) to hold back

survivor (sər vī´ vər) one who lives through a disaster

suspicious (səs pĭsh´ əs) arousing distrust

sympathetic (sĭm´ pə thĕt´ ĭk) feeling sorry for something or someone

tangle (tăng´ gl) to mix together

task (tăsk) a job; assigned work

tattered (tăt´ ərd) torn or ragged

tedious (tē´ dē əs or tē´ jəs) tiresome, boring

thorough (thĕr´ ō) complete; painstakingly careful

threaten (thrĕt´ n) endanger

tingle (tĭng´ gl) a slight stinging sensation

tolerant (tŏl´ ər ənt) patient; able to accept the belief of others

tolerate (tŏl´ ər āt) to allow without opposing

torrent (tôr´ ənt) turbulent or overwhelming flood

tremble (trĕm´ bl) to shake or shiver involuntarily

triumphant (trī ŭm´ fənt) victorious; successful

trudge (trŭj) to walk in a heavy way; plod

unbearable (ŭn bâr´ ə bl) not able to be endured; intolerable

unfortunate (ŭn fôr´ chə nĭt) unlucky; characterized by bad fortune

unintentional (ŭn´ ĭn tĕn´ shə nl) not done or said on purpose

unjust (ŭn jŭst´) unfair

unreasonable (ŭn rē´ zn ə bl) not reasonable; exceeding normal limits

unruly (ŭn rü´ lē) difficult to control

unsteady (ŭn stĕd´ ē) unstable; wavering; changeable

unusual (ŭn ū´ zhü əl) uncommon; not ordinary

urge (ĕrj) to push, to force or drive onward; encourage

various (vâr´ ē əs) more than one; of several kinds

vast (văst) very great in area, intensity, size, or amount

vicinity (və sĭn´ ə tē) a nearby or surrounding region or place

visible (vĭz´ ə bl) able to be seen

wage (wāj) to engage in or carry on

warrant (wôr´ ənt) a written order for arrest, search, or seizure

wearily (wĭr´ ə lē) tired, worn out

welcome (wĕl´ kəm) to greet or receive

yearning (yĕr´ nĭng) a deep longing; desire

yelp (yĕlp) to bark sharply

Notes

Studying
Vocabulary

1

PRESTWICK HOUSE, INC.

"Everything for the English Classroom!"

1-800-932-4593 • www.prestwickhouse.com

Reorder No. SV50A

ISBN 1-58049-250-9

9 781580 492508

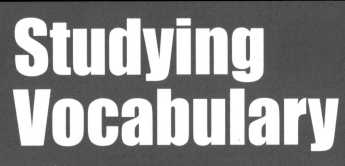

PRESTWICK HOUSE, INC.

Studying Vocabulary

2

Advanced